1

MAKING IN AMERICA:
U.S. Manufacturing Entrepreneurship and Innovation

Innovation is central to continued American opportunity and prosperity – raising our standard of living and launching new industries. American manufacturing, which contributes the vast majority of U.S. private sector research and development, is central to American innovation, both to discoveries being made today and our ability to drive productivity growth and discover new technologies in the future.

From 2000 to 2010, U.S. manufacturing production and investment in new capacity stagnated, resulting in the offshoring and shuttering of thousands of American factories and the loss of millions of jobs, raising doubts about the future of manufacturing's contribution to American innovation. Since the end of the recession, U.S. manufacturing is once again on the upswing, buoyed by the United States' growing competitiveness for manufacturing jobs and investment.

With this strengthening of U.S. manufacturing has come a fundamental strengthening of America's innovation enterprise. At the same time, emerging manufacturing technologies are introducing a new source of advantage for U.S. manufacturing, spurring entrepreneurship in U.S. manufacturing by re-connecting our historical leadership in invention and innovation with our growing competitiveness in production.

U.S. manufacturing plays an outsized role in supporting and driving American innovation, and increasingly our ability to manufacture undergirds our future ability to innovate:

- Manufacturing represents 12 percent of U.S. GDP, but it contributes 60% of all U.S. research and development employees, 75% of U.S. private sector research and development, and the vast majority of all patents issued in the United States.[1]

- U.S. manufacturing firms are more innovative, on average, innovating at more than twice the rate of other U.S. businesses – with over 30% reporting an innovation between 2008 and 2010 alone compared to only 13% for other U.S. businesses.[2]

- For many technologies, the capabilities gained in production are intertwined with new learning and the knowledge activities of research, development and design. The iterative innovation cycle between engineering and production on the shop floor is responsible for a range of breakthrough technologies, explaining why firms are increasingly reconnecting production with development and design.[3]

U.S. manufacturing is more competitive than it has been in decades:

- Manufacturing output has increased 30% since the end of the recession, growing at roughly twice the pace of the economy overall, marking the longest period where manufacturing has outpaced U.S. economic output since 1965.[4]

- Since February 2010, the United States has directly added 646,000 manufacturing jobs, with the sector expanding employment at its fastest rate in nearly two decades. [5] In addition, manufacturing supports millions of additional jobs across its supply chain and in the communities in which it locates.[6]

- Due to a highly productive workforce, sizeable and transparent markets, low-cost energy, and our historic lead in innovation, the United States is once again the leading destination for business investment. Global executives surveyed by AT Kearney across all industries and geographies ranked the U.S. #1 as the destination for business investment.[7]

- The United States' renewed competitiveness in manufacturing is luring production back. 54% of U.S.-based manufacturers surveyed by The Boston Consulting Group are actively considering bringing production back from China to the United States, up from 37% only 18 months prior. [8]

New technologies are lowering the cost and reducing the time required for businesses and entrepreneurs to design, test, and produce new products, creating a new source of advantage for U.S. manufacturing.

- *Rapid and low-cost prototyping*: New technologies for rapid prototyping – from laser cutters to CNC routers to 3D printers – have dramatically lowered the cost of developing a prototype. The ability to rapidly and affordably test, tinker, monitor and customize places a premium on locating close to American markets and opens new doors to entrepreneurship and innovation in manufacturing. Access to these tools is inspiring a new movement of Makers, inventors, and entrepreneurs.

- *Digital design and devices:* The nation's historic strengths in software and digital design – the U.S. produces 80% of the world's software, leads in "big data" analytics and sensors, and contains the majority of the world's supercomputing – are positioning it to lead in an era of connected devices and of products that are digitally designed, tested, and assembled before taking final form on the shop floor.[9]

The results of these emerging technologies and renewed focus on manufacturing innovation are already spurring change in U.S. manufacturing. Existing manufacturers have accelerated investment in research and development while the rate of growth for entrepreneurs opening new businesses in manufacturing is at its fastest pace in over 20 years.

Existing manufacturers are accelerating investment in U.S. innovation:

- American manufacturers have accelerated investments in R&D in the United States. Already globally the largest source of manufacturing R&D, the R&D intensity of U.S. manufacturing since 2003 has also grown faster than that of any other country save South Korea, growing from 8% to nearly 11%.[10]

- Manufacturing R&D investment in the U.S. is now at an all-time high at $202 billion, or 75% of total U.S. private sector R&D.[11]

- Manufacturing firms at the forefront of new technologies have particularly increased their investment, with, for instance, the precision machining industry growing its investment in U.S. R&D by 48% or nearly $5B between 2010 and 2011 alone.[12]

- Established manufacturers, such as Ford and GE, are taking advantage of new technologies like rapid prototyping networks to develop new products. Ford's partnership with TechShop, a membership-based fabrication and prototyping center open to the public, credited with a more than 50% increase in patenting among Ford's engineers at their global R&D headquarters in Dearborn, MI in just two years.[13] GE, which re-shored its appliance manufacturing in order to more rapidly take innovative products to market, is sourcing new designs and ideas from Local Motors' Microfactories, shop-sized, local factories designed to go from design to production in a space the size of the average garage.

Entrepreneurs are starting new manufacturing firms at fastest rate in two decades:

- The growth rate of new manufacturing firms, a leading indicator of entrepreneurship, is at its fastest pace since 1993.[14]

- And for the first time since 1999, the number of manufacturing establishments is growing as new companies form and existing companies branch out into new factories, with more than 1,400 new establishments opening in 2013.[15] And this expansion is widely spread across 19 out of 21 major manufacturing industries – occurring in industries as diverse as chemicals, electronics and machinery. [16]

- Rapid prototyping networks are providing platforms for new entrepreneurship. For example, Shapeways, a 3D printing service and online marketplace has launched over 16,000 online shops, 94% of which spent less than $1,000 to produce and market their first products.

- A national movement is brewing of Makers, tinkerers, and inventors who are scaling up from DIY to Made in the USA through networks and platforms like Etsy, Tindie, Indeigogo, Quirky, Grommet, and Kickstarter.

To augment and capture this new source of advantage from U.S. manufacturing innovation and entrepreneurship, the Administration has made spurring innovation in U.S. manufacturing a core priority of its manufacturing agenda. The Administration has increased federal investment in manufacturing R&D by 35% from $1.4B in 2011 to $1.9B in 2014.[17] Through the National Network for Manufacturing Innovation – with four hubs already and four more on the way – the Administration is bringing together private industry, leading universities, and federal agencies to co-invest in emerging technologies like additive manufacturing, lightweight materials, next-generation power electronics, and digital design and fabrication. Later this week, the Administration will announce new investments in materials technologies critical for future production and efforts to facilitate access to the federal government's world leading equipment and infrastructure for manufacturers. Through these investments and a continued focus on strengthening domestic production, the Administration is laying the foundation for a revitalization of American manufacturing, shoring up the central pillar of America's innovation enterprise.

MANUFACTURING ANCHORS THE INNOVATION ECONOMY

American innovation has long been central to humanity's ability to address our most critical challenges while making current and future generations of Americans better off than their forebears. The development of new ideas, new technologies, new products, and new ways of working have raised American productivity, expanded our economy, and improved our quality of life. The U.S. manufacturing sector lies at the heart of the American innovation economy.

For many reasons, the Administration has made strengthening our manufacturing sector a priority – manufacturing consistently leads to well-paying jobs that pay 16% more overall than average[18], it drives the majority of our exports, and it spurs jobs-growth in the communities where it locates and throughout its supply chains, from the lab to the factory floor and out onto the loading dock.

Total Compensation Premium, Manufacturing vs. Other Industries (Percent, 2000 to 2011)

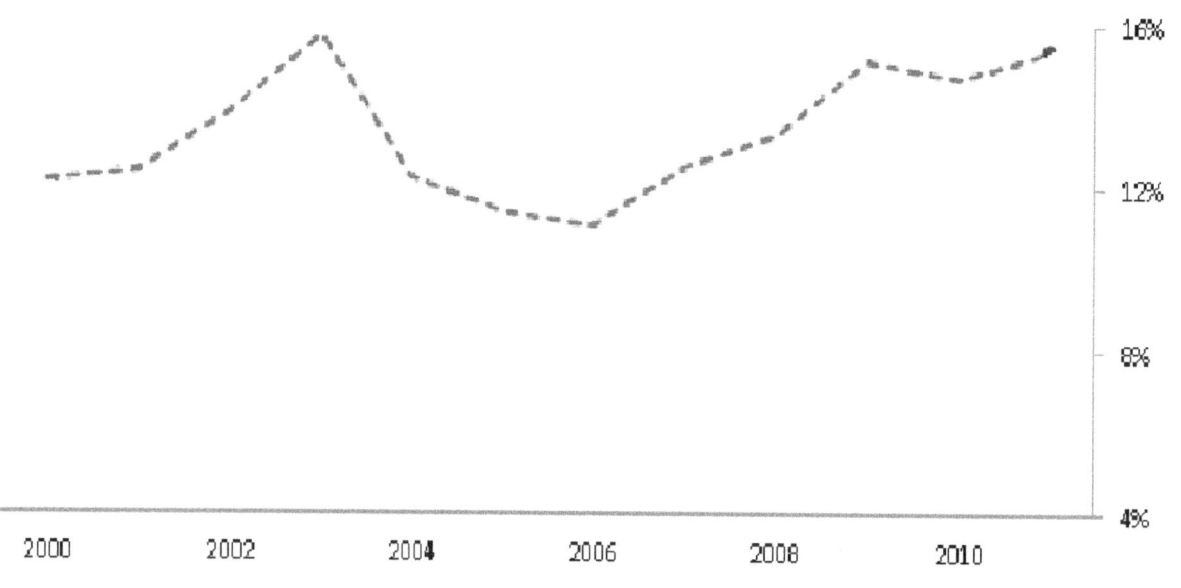

Source: Economics and Statistical Administration, Department of Commerce; Regression results controlling for demographic, geographic, and educational characteristic; private wage and hourly workers

But, perhaps most of all, manufacturing matters because of its outsized role in anchoring and fueling the American innovation economy. Manufacturing, while accounting for just 12% of GDP, makes up 60% of all private sector U.S. research and development employees, and contributes 75% of private sector research and development.[19,20]

Manufacturing firms in the U.S. innovate at a rate two times that of other U.S. businesses – over 30% of U.S. manufacturers reported an innovation – the introduction

6

of a radically new product or process – in 2010, compared to only 13% of other businesses.[21] High-tech manufacturers report even higher rates of product and process innovation. Manufacturers of communications equipment, aircraft and spacecraft, pharmaceuticals, and computers, for example, report rates of innovation that are at least double the U.S. manufacturing sector average.[22]

Companies Introducing a New Product or Process Innovation (Percent, 2008 to 2010)

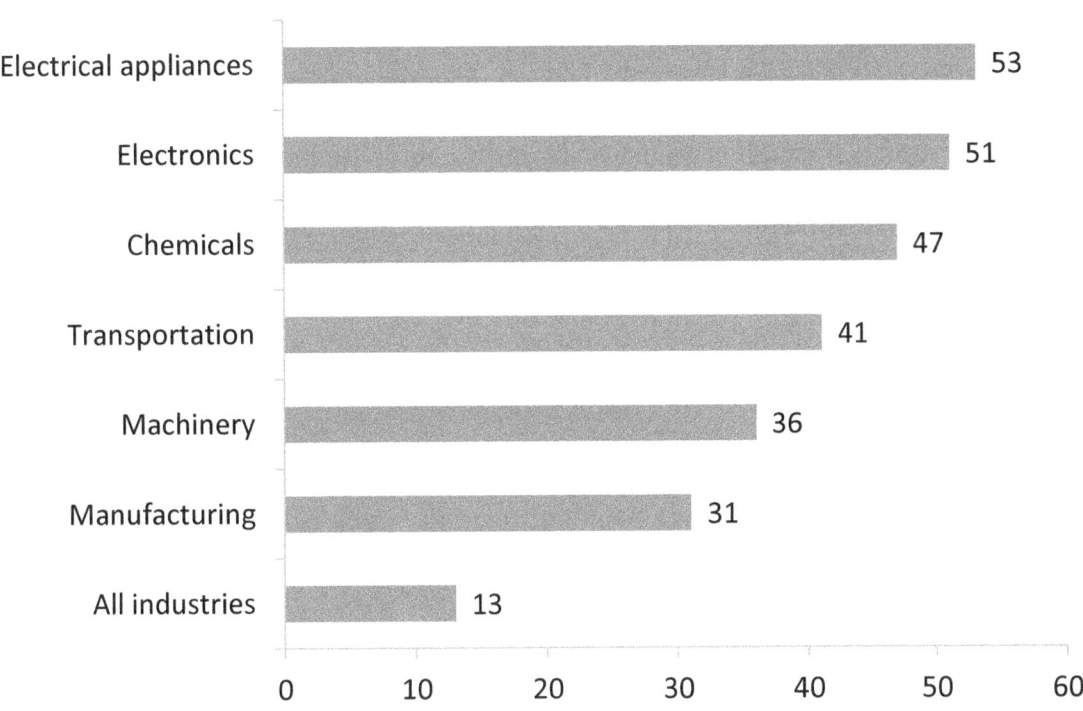

Source: National Science Foundation, Science and Engineering Indicators

Innovations in manufacturing have important spillover benefits for innovations and employment in other industries. Businesses downstream from innovative U.S. manufacturers benefit from lower costs and improved processes, which in turn allow them to increase investment and employment. Studies have shown that knowledge spillovers for the broader economy increase with proximity to manufacturing and manufacturing's investments in research and development.[23]

Finally, it is increasingly understood that not only our strengths today, but our future strengths in innovation as well, depend on retaining the knowledge and knowhow that come from manufacturing here. As the MIT Production in the Innovation Economy commission concluded, the proximity of manufacturing and research is important because "learning takes place as engineers and technicians on the factory floor come back with their problems to the design engineers and struggle with them to find better resolutions; learning takes place as users come back with problems."[24]

The link between production and innovation is the reason many credit Intel's four-to-five-year technology lead with the firm's decision to locate its chip manufacturing near its design facilities in the United States and why that famed fount of 20th century innovation, Bell Labs, "housed thinkers and doers under one roof". The knowledge gleaned from one generation of technologies, and often the iterative process and specialized knowledge required to produce them, generate important insights for discovering the next.

U.S. MANUFACTURING'S RESURGENCE

From 2000 to 2010, American production and investment in new capacity stagnated. Tens of thousands of manufacturing factories closed down. The manufacturing sector lost millions of jobs. The challenges faced by manufacturing led to concerns that the engine of American innovation was at risk. As companies shipped production overseas, important knowledge and capabilities left. Some, including Willy Shih and Gary Pisano of Harvard Business School, warned that the loss of production during this period in American-invented technologies such as flat-screen TVs and lithium batteries threatened our ability to either invent or make the next generation of technologies.[25]

Since the end of the recession, manufacturing in America has become a bright spot of the recovery, adding jobs and expanding at an historic rate thanks to increased U.S. competitiveness for jobs and investment. Manufacturing output has increased 30% since the end of the recession, growing at roughly twice the pace of the economy overall, the longest period during which manufacturing has outpaced U.S. economic output since 1965.[26]

Since February 2010, the United States has directly added 646,000 manufacturing jobs, with the sector expanding employment at its fastest rate in nearly two decades.[27] In addition, this renewed growth in manufacturing has created millions of additional jobs across its supply chain and in the communities where it locates. Researchers estimate that for every job created in manufacturing, an additional 1.6 jobs open in the broader economy.[28]

There are signs that this expansion in manufacturing could accelerate. Average annual weekly hours for production workers in the manufacturing sector have climbed to 42.1, the highest level since 1945.[29] As Barclays posits in its recent analysis, this historically high level of hours suggests pent up demand among manufacturers for workers and expansion.[30]

Avg. Weekly Hours for Manufacturing Production Workers, 2000 to 2013

Source: Bureau of Labor Statistics, Current Employment Statistics Survey

A surge in U.S. competitiveness for jobs and investment in manufacturing lies at the heart of this renaissance in American manufacturing. As Bridgewater, a leading global investment fund, has observed, the United States is at "its strongest competitive position in over a decade".[31] In AT Kearney's 2013 FDI Confidence Index, the United States surged past countries like China, Brazil and India to become the country with the top FDI prospects globally, as ranked by 302 companies representing 28 countries and multiple industry sectors.[32] This marks the first time that the US occupied the #1 spot in the survey since 2001.[33] Earlier this month, the United States' lengthened its lead on the 2014 AT Kearney survey of global investment – scoring the highest out of all countries for investment from across all geographies and industries, including manufacturing.

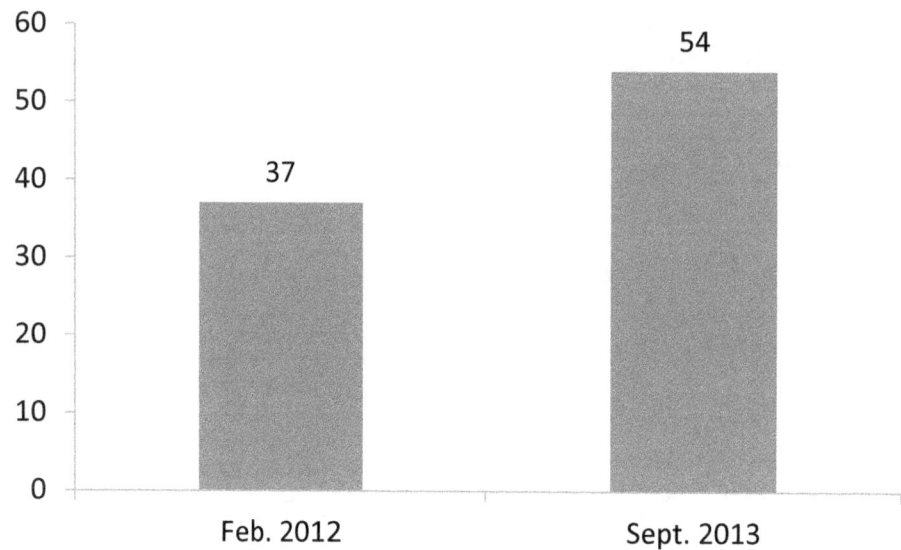

Manufacturers Considering Moving from China to the United States (Percent, >$ 1 billion in revenues)

Source: The Boston Consulting Group

As a result of this competitiveness, manufacturers – like Whirlpool, Masterlock, K'NEX, Ford, and more are expanding and bringing production back to the United States. In a survey of U.S. manufacturers with production abroad late last year, BCG found that the majority (54 percent) are looking at re-shoring to the United States, up from 37 percent in 2012. [34]

The rising competitiveness of U.S. manufacturing is driven by the deep skills and productivity of our workforce, our expansive and low-cost energy resources, the unparalleled size of our markets, and our historic strengths in innovation.

The U.S. workforce is among the most skilled and productive globally – more than 30 percent more productive than Germany's and nearly twice as productive as South Korea's.[35] With a century of reserves, natural gas costs one third as much here as it does in Asia and our low energy costs overall are estimated to save U.S. manufacturers nearly $130 billion annually compared to Europe.[36]

Natural Gas Prices in the United States, United Kingdom, and Japan ($ per million Btu)

Source: McKinsey Global Institute

Locating in the United States provides unparalleled access to the largest consumer market in the world and rapid access to global markets, with the United States having free trade agreements with 20 other countries and the most rapid export clearances of the 185 countries surveyed by the World Bank.[37]

And the United States continues to lead the world in innovation. The United States is the global leader in patents, producing nearly 30 percent of all patents worldwide, and has 15 of the top 25 leading research universities.[38] Not surprisingly, the United States also has over a third of the world's total R&D investment, more than any other country.[39] In fact, the United States invests twice as much as any other nation in research and development – spending $429 billion in 2011, far more than China's $208 billion or Japan's $146 billion.[40]

NEW TECHNOLOGIES STRENGTHENING OUR EDGE FOR MANUFACTURING INNOVATION AND INVESTMENT

In addition to the United States' competitive advantages for investment, new technologies and advances in manufacturing design and production create new advantages for manufacturing production and investment in the United States. Digitally-enabled manufacturing technologies – such as connected devices, digital design and testing, and 3D printing – play to U.S. strengths in software and computing. And the increasingly affordable and available technologies for rapid prototyping enable mass customization, placing a premium on access to markets, and can spur a new generation of startups in manufacturing. By opening up new avenues of possibility and lowering the barriers to entry for new entrepreneurs and innovators in manufacturing, these technologies can accelerate U.S. manufacturing innovation.

Low-cost Prototyping

New tools, technologies, and platforms are making it faster and cheaper to prototype products, creating novel opportunities for entrepreneurship in manufacturing in the United States. For example:

- Additive manufacturing, also known as 3D printing and scanning, can reduce the cost of designing and prototyping automobile components by as much as 99%[41]

- Do-It-Yourself (DIY) electronics kits and low-cost microcontroller sets, like those produced by Arduino, Sparkfun or Adafruit, can power complex electronic gadgets ranging from cell phones to satellites

- New online platforms and communities can help entrepreneurs rapidly assemble the talent they need – be it finding engineers on Instructables or crowdsourcing design wisdom from Grommet

The new technologies can dramatically lower the cost of prototyping in manufacturing, costs that historically have been a barrier to manufacturing startups and to rapid customization at established companies. Take 3D printing at Ford for example. Using traditional injection-molding methods, a prototype of an intake manifold — the most complicated part of an engine — takes about four months and $500,000 for Ford to create. In contrast, by using additive manufacturing technology, Ford can print the same part in four days, with multiple iterations and no tooling limits, for $3,000.[42] These cost savings can be especially meaningful for manufacturing startups – like Peppermint Energy, a solar energy devices company, which saved $250,000 in tooling costs through the use of 3D printing, compared with traditional mold-based techniques.[43]

Another example of a sector that is leveraging new technologies that speed the design-build-test cycle is biomanufacturing. For example, a conventional process takes at least six months to generate vaccines ready for use, far too slow to halt the advance of a pandemic. Using new capabilities in biomanufacturing, researchers showed that they could shave weeks off the time needed for vaccine manufacture, potentially saving countless lives.[44]

And these technologies are becoming both cheaper and more widely available. Sales of personal 3D printers grew 200% to 400% each year between 2007 and 2011, while the cost of a high-end personal 3D printer fell from over $4,000 to $1,500, with further cost declines expected.[45] Increasingly, the price of desktop 3D printers continues to drop, with the Micro 3D Printer priced at $299 and other, even lower-cost models coming to market. Similarly, the costs of microcontroller boards have fallen from over $100 in 2005 to less than $10 in 2014. The number of Arduino boards sold, just one example of these devices, more than doubled between 2011 and 2013 to over 700,000 boards.[46]

Many of these tools are being improved upon by the Makers who use them through open-source tools and platforms, like Arduino's programming platform, or through modifications made by a growing community of Makers, like those that led to MakerBot's low-cost personal 3D printers.

TechShop

Self-described as a "playground for creativity" and "part fabrication and prototyping studio, part hackerspace and part learning center,"[47] TechShop is a chain of workshops where individuals can take classes on electronics, metal working, and other industrial tool-based skills and use the space and equipment to build and test their own products.

With eight locations around the United States and more on the way, TechShop serves as a workspace not only for hobbyists and students but also for start-ups that are looking to reduce tooling costs. Standing at the intersection of manufacturing and innovation, the company aims to support what CEO Mark Hatch sees as the upcoming revolution in small-scale, niche manufacturing.[48]

One of the most well-known products to have come out of TechShop is Square, a device that allows smartphones and tablets to be used as credit-card readers. In 2009, inventors Jim McKelvey and Jack Dorsey first built a prototype for Square at the TechShop in Menlo Park, California.[49] Since then, the company has grown to over 600 employees and a full office in San Francisco.[50]

Similarly, DODOCase, a company that produces custom iPad cases made of bamboo and bookbinding, was first built at the Menlo Park TechShop by Patrick Buckley. Initially, Buckley was an aspiring "maker" who did not know how to use wood working tools to create the retro cases he had envisioned. But he managed to design his product after learning how to cut up and connect sheets of bamboo at TechShop, and within one year, Buckley had sold about $4 million of DODOCases. By May 2012, his company employed 25 people and had a factory in San Francisco.[51]

In addition to the rise of these tools for personal use – networks of makerspaces and mini-factories across the country – such as TechShop, Fablab, NextFab, Local Motors Microfactories, and more – are opening up access to the latest equipment for prototyping and small batch manufacturing. Alongside access to cutting edge tools and technology, members can also access experts knowledgeable in using these machines who are willing to share their expertise with others.

The rapid development cycles and reduced costs enabled by these tools make it even more attractive to locate near the United States' large domestic market in order to meet changing consumer tastes. As product cycles shorten, for all but the highest value products that firms can afford to ship by air, proximity to the customer will be paramount for companies seeking to hit store shelves before their competitors. Wal-Mart credits this proximity to its customers for part of its decision to bring back $50 billion in production to the United States.

And as these technologies make it cheaper and easier for inventors and entrepreneurs to produce their first products and prototypes they have the potential to unlock a wave of manufacturing innovation and entrepreneurship. Comparisons with software innovation abound. As Chris Anderson, a former editor of WIRED magazine, puts it "Three guys with laptops used to describe a Web startup. Now it describes a hardware company, too."[52]

Digital Design & Connected Devices

The United States' strengths in digital design and software development are positioning us for new innovations in connected devices and the integration of digital design with manufacturing. As of November 2013, the United States has 264 of the top 500 most powerful high performance computer systems (HPCs) in the world. The United States is the most advanced country for software development, with 80% of the world's software is produced in the United States.[53]

Today, software development is a critical component of each step of the manufacturing process: product design, production planning, engineering, execution, and service.[54] High performance computers give U.S. manufacturers the ability to model designs in the virtual world and then simulate them. To this end, designers can test countless ideas and tweak them until finally reaching that optimal product design.[55] For entrepreneurs, software and high performance computing significantly reduce the barriers to entry into capital intensive industries where significant time and capital are normally required to prototype and test.

Further, trends such as big data and analytics will provide real-time advantages to the manufacturing floor and the supply chain by providing visibility and increased communication throughout the value chain. For example, in the 1980s, Boeing tested 77 prototypes of its 767 using wind tunnels. By 2005, Boeing ran only 11 tests for its 787, testing prototypes using virtual wind tunnels and supercomputing.[56]

Engineers at GE are working with Arizona State and Cornell universities to make more efficient jet engines, using the supercomputers Sierra and Titan to examine the design of fuel injectors. With a combined computing power of 10,000 processors operating simultaneously over 9 months, GE can experiment with slight changes in design to discover which minor modifications will most increase engine power and fuel efficiency while reducing emissions.[57]

In addition, in a world where almost any manufactured product from cars to cell phones to jet engines to wheelchairs can become a "digital device", the United States' combined strengths in manufacturing and software innovation position us to capture more production of cutting edge, digitally-enabled devices. For example, the Chevy Volt contains over 10 million lines of software code, and software developer is one of the fastest growing technical professions in Southeast Michigan, a region long known for its manufacturing prowess.[58]

Early stage hardware startups like BioMeme, producer of a smartphone docking station that can process DNA tests, and Love Park Robotics, which supplies the sensors for self-navigating electric wheelchairs, integrate hardware and software innovations in their devices. And the range of physical products whose hardware elements become integral platforms for software applications is expanding. Already, nine billion devices are connected to the internet with some expecting that number to increase to more than 50 billion in the next ten years.[59]

These new technologies for the integration of software with "connected or digital devices" and with the whole of manufacturing processes and design play to existing U.S. strengths in software given the "co-location synergies between the developers of hardware and software and the high-tech services that integrate these components into the system that provides the service to customers."[60]

These innovations in rapid prototyping and design are especially effective when paired with the United States' deep expertise in machining, metal working, and established manufacturing base. Groups like FuzeHub in New York and the Manufacturing Extension Partnership with its national Supplier Scouting network are helping new startups go from DIY to Made in the USA by connecting them with established U.S. contract manufacturers who can take their prototypes into full scale production.

A NEW WAVE OF MANUFACTURING INNOVATION AND ENTREPRENEURSHIP EMERGING

The United States' increasing competitiveness for manufacturing jobs and investment, our historic strengths in innovation, and the rise of new technologies that make it easier than ever to invent and make are spurring investment in U.S. innovation and a new wave of entrepreneurship in manufacturing. Manufacturers are intensifying their investments in U.S. innovation and manufacturing is adding factories for the first time since 1999.

To capture the advantages of American innovation, U.S. manufacturers have been intensifying their investment in research and development in the United States. Already the largest source globally of manufacturing research and development, U.S. manufacturing research and development, as a percent of overall manufacturing sales, since 2003 has intensified faster than in any other country save South Korea.[61]

Manufacturers now invest $202 billion in U.S. research and development annually, at an all-time high, up more than 50% or $68 billion since 2004 when manufacturing investments in U.S. research first accelerated.[62] Manufacturing now accounts for 75% of all U.S. private sector research and development.[63]

Manufacturing firms at the forefront of new technologies have particularly increased their investment in recent years. For example, the precision machining industry increased its investment in U.S. R&D by48% or nearly $5B between 2010 and 2011 alone.[64] And the

U.S. semiconductor industry has increased by 52% its investment in US R&D, a total increase of $10 billion, between 2007 and 2012 alone.[65]

Manufacturing Private Fixed Investment in R&D
(Billions, 2000 to 2012)

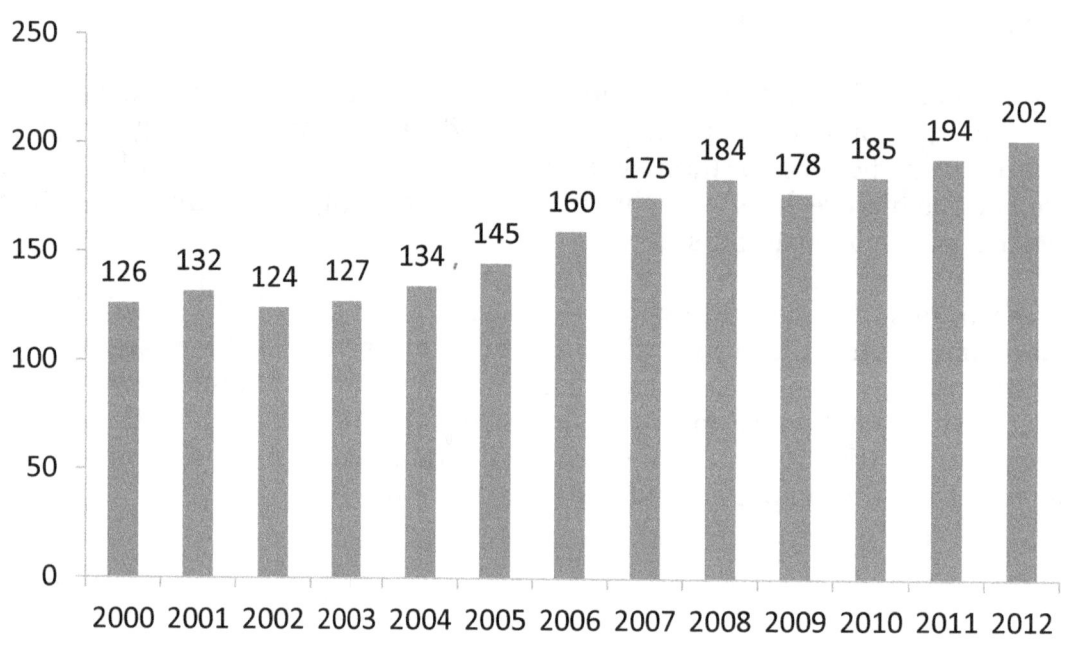

Source: Bureau of Economic Analysis

In addition to increasing their investment in research and development, established manufacturers, like Ford and GE, are taking advantage of new technologies like rapid prototyping networks to develop new products. Ford's partnership with TechShop, a membership-based fabrication and prototyping center, led to a more than 50% increase in patenting among Ford's engineers at its R&D headquarters in Dearborn, MI in just two years. GE, which re-shored its appliance manufacturing in order to more rapidly take innovative products to market, is sourcing new designs and ideas from Local Motors' Microfactories, which are shop-sized, local factories designed to go from design to production in the space of a typical garage.

In addition to intensifying investments in U.S. research and development, new technologies, access to prototyping, and an increasingly attractive environment for manufacturing are leading to an upswing in manufacturing entrepreneurship. For the first time in over fifteen years, manufacturing entrepreneurs have turned the corner and are opening up new shops.

At the end of 2011, the growth rate of new firm creation in manufacturing, a leading indicator of entrepreneurship, reached its highest levels since 1993, growing 6% year over year.

Entrepreneurship in manufacturing is on an upswing – with the number of new firms opening up shop growing at its fastest rate since 1993, with a 6% increase in 2011 over the previous year.[66] All signs suggest that subsequent data releases will show a strengthening of this trend.

In 2013, for the first time since 1999, the number of manufacturing establishments is growing as new companies form and existing companies branch out into new factories, with more than 1,400 new establishments opening. The growth in manufacturing establishments is widely spread across 19 out of 21 major manufacturing industries – occurring in industries as diverse as chemicals, electronics and machinery.[67]

In addition to new technologies, new online platforms, such as rapid prototyping networks, are providing opportunities for new entrepreneurship in manufacturing. For example, Shapeways, a 3D printing service and online marketplace has launched over 16,000 online sellers, 94% of which spent less than $1,000 to produce and market their first products.[68] And fundraising platforms are helping manufacturers access more capital. At one Maker Faire alone, manufacturing or "Maker" projects raised over $26 million from donors on Kickstarter, allowing them to launch more than 100 new products.[69]

Meanwhile, partnerships between design platforms like Quirky and major retailers like Home Depot, Walgreens, and Target are creating new opportunities for early-stage manufacturing companies to see their products on shelves nationwide. Able to help its members take a product from design to retail in just four months, Quirky has already helped manufacturing entrepreneurs in its network reach more than 30,000 doors.[70]

To capture and augment this new advantage for U.S. manufacturing innovation and entrepreneurship, the Administration has made spurring innovation in U.S. manufacturing a core priority of its manufacturing agenda.

Through the National Network for Manufacturing Innovation – with four hubs already established and four more on the way – the Administration is bringing together private industry, leading universities, and federal agencies to co-invest in emerging technologies like additive manufacturing, lightweight materials, next-generation power electronics, and digital design and fabrication.

Each institute is designed to serve as a regional hub bridging the gap between applied research and product development, bringing together companies, universities and other academic and training institutions, and Federal agencies to co-invest in technology areas that encourage investment and production in the United States. This type of "teaching factory" provides a unique opportunity for educating and training students and workers at all levels, while providing the shared assets to help companies, most importantly small manufacturers, access cutting-edge capabilities and equipment to design, test, and pilot new products and manufacturing processes.

The Administration has increased federal investment in manufacturing R&D by 35% from $1.4B in 2011 to $1.9B in 2014.[71] And, in calling on Congress to increase overall U.S. leadership in research and development by restoring our national investments in research and development to the world-leading heights attained during the space race, the President has laid out an ambitious agenda to sustain our lead in innovation.

Small and medium-sized manufacturers are both essential to the competitiveness of U.S. supply chains, yet they too often lag larger firms in innovation and in adopting the latest technologies. For example, a 2011 Case Western University survey found that one-third of auto suppliers did not perform any R&D, and 40% had zero engineers.[72] Recognizing this fact, the Administration has made strengthening and expanding the Manufacturing Extension Partnership a core priority, calling on Congress to expand the program's budget while intensifying the MEP's outreach to and support of small and medium manufacturing firms. The MEP is a nationwide system of centers in every state, and engages over 30,000 small and medium manufacturers annually to overcome the challenges faced by firms in the commercialization of the latest technologies.

In addition, later this week, the Administration will announce its latest efforts to promote innovation in manufacturing and to provide entrepreneurs with access to leading edge tools to develop and deploy new products. The Administration will be stepping up its investments in cutting edge materials and partnering with the private sector to see these materials go into production through a $150 million investment in the Materials Genome Initiative. By providing better data on the location and availability of cutting-edge research equipment, the Administration will be facilitating access to over $5 billion in equipment for manufacturing entrepreneurs. Through this effort, entrepreneurs will gain access to facilities like NASA's National Center for Advanced Manufacturing to produce the high-strength, defect-free joints required for cutting-edge aeronautics, or DOE's Manufacturing Demonstration Facility at Oak Ridge National Laboratory for collaborative projects in additive manufacturing, composites and carbon fiber, and other leading clean energy technologies.

Through these investments and a continued focus on strengthening domestic production, the Administration is laying the foundation for a revitalization of American manufacturing, shoring up the central pillar of America's innovation enterprise.

[1] Bureau of Economic Analysis, Department of Commerce
[2] National Science Foundation, Science and Engineering Indicators.
[3] MIT Production in the Innovation Economy Commission. *Production in the Innovation Economy*, 2013.
[4] Bureau of Economic Analysis, Department of Commerce, NIPA tables
[5] Bureau of Labor Statistics, Department of Labor, Current Employment Statistics Survey
[6] McKinsey Global Institute. *Manufacturing the Future.* November 2012.
[7] AT Kearney. Foreign Direct Investment Confidence Index, 2014.
[8] Boston Consulting Group. Majority of Large Manufacturers Are Now Planning or Considering 'Reshoring' from China to the U.S. http://www.bcg.com/media/pressreleasedetails.aspx?id=tcm:12-144944.
[9] Top500 project. Top500 Supercomputer sites. 2014. http://www.top500.org/.
[10] Tassey, Gregory. *Rationales and mechanisms for revitalizing US Manufacturing R&D strategies.* NIST, 2010
[11] Bureau of Economic Analysis, Department of Commerce
[12] National Science Foundation, Science and Engineering Indicators.
[13] Interviews with Ford senior executives.
[14] U.S. Census, Business Dynamics Statistics.
[15] Bureau of Labor Statistics, Department of Labor.
[16] Bureau of Labor Statistics, Department of Labor.
[17] Office of Management and Budget. Manufacturing Research and Development cross-cut, 2014.
[18] U.S. Department of Commerce, Economics and Statistics Administration. *The Benefits of Manufacturing Jobs.* May 2012.
[19] Bureau of Economic Analysis, Department of commerce
[20] National Science Foundation National Center for Science and Engineering Statistics and U.S. Census Bureau, Business R&D and Innovation Survey, 2010
[21] National Science Foundation National Center for Science and Engineering Statistics and U.S. Census Bureau, Business R&D and Innovation Survey, 2010
[22] National Science Foundation National Center for Science and Engineering Statistics. Science and Engineering Indicators, 2014
[23] Keller, Wolfgang. "Geographic Localization Of International Technology Diffusion," American Economic Review, 2002, v92(1,Mar), 120-142. ; Branstetter, Lee. "Are Knowledge Spillovers International or Intranational in Scope? Microeconometric
[24] MIT Taskforce on Production in the Innovation Economy. *Preview of the MIT Production in the Innovation Economy Report.* February 2013.
[25] Pisano, Gary and Willy Shih. Restoring American Competitiveness. July 2009.
[26] Bureau of Economic Analysis, Department of Commerce
[27] Bureau of Labor Statistics, Department of Labor
[28] Moretti, Enrico. "Local Multipliers." *American Economic Review: Papers & Proceedings 100 (May 2010): 1–7.*
[29] Bureau of Labor Statistics, Department of Labor
[30] Barclays. Manufacturing Employment Outlook: Manufacturing a Turnaround. December 2013
[31] Bridgewater Daily Observations. *The Ongoing US Energy Boom and Manufacturing Renaissance.* June 6, 2014.
[32] AT Kearney, Foreign Direct Investment Confidence Index, 2013 & 2014
[33] Ibid.

[34] Boston Consulting Group. Majority of Large Manufacturers Are Now Planning or Considering 'Reshoring' from China to the U.S. http://www.bcg.com/media/pressreleasedetails.aspx?id=tcm:12-144944.

[35] The Conference Board Total Economy Database™, January 2014, http://www.conference-board.org/data/economydatabase/

[36] McKinsey Global Institute. *Game Changers: Five opportunities for U.S. Growth and Renewal.* July 2013.; World Energy Outlook 2013 Factsheet. http://www.iea.org/media/files/WEO2013_factsheets.pdf.

[37] World Bank. Doing Business Project. *Time to Export.* http://data.worldbank.org/indicator/IC.EXP.DURS

[38] World Intellectual Property Organization. Press Release March 2014. http://www.wipo.int/pressroom/en/articles/2014/article_0002.html.; Times Higher Education World Reputation Rankings 2014. http://www.theguardian.com/news/datablog/2014/mar/06/worlds-top-100-universities-2014-reputations-ranked-times-higher-education.

[39] Batelle. Global R&D Funding Forecast 2014. www.battelle.org

[40] National Science Foundation, National Center for Science and Engineering Statistics, *Science and Engineering Indicators 2014.*

[41] Ford Press Release, "Ford's 3D-Printed Auto Parts Save Millions, Boost Quality," December 12, 2013." https://media.ford.com/content/fordmedia/fna/us/en/news/2013/12/12/ford_s-3d-printed-auto-parts-save-millions--boost-quality.html.

[42] Ford Press Release, "Ford's 3D-Printed Auto Parts Save Millions, Boost Quality," December 12, 2013." https://media.ford.com/content/fordmedia/fna/us/en/news/2013/12/12/ford_s-3d-printed-auto-parts-save-millions--boost-quality.html.

[43] Stratasys Case Studies. Peppermint Energy: 3D Printing Helps Solar Upstart Deliver Energy Everywhere. www.stratasys.com/resources/case-studies/consumer-goods/peppermint-energy.

[44] Dormitzer, PR., *et al., Synthetic Generation of Influenza Vaccine Viruses for Rapid Response to Pandemics.* Science Translational Medicine 5, 185ra68, 2013.

[45] McKinsey Global Institute, "Disruptive technologies: Advances that will transform life, business, and the global economy," May 2013.

[46] http://medea.mah.se/2013/04/arduino-faq/

[47] TechShop. http://techshop.ws/.

[48] Washington Post, "With TechShop, the maker movement begins its rise in Washington," April 6, 2014, http://www.washingtonpost.com/news/capital-business/wp/2014/04/06/maker-movement-begins-rise-washington/.

[49] RiverFront Times, "High-Tech Workshop Where Jack Dorsey and Jim McKelvey Built Square Eyeing St. Louis," February 27, 2014. http://blogs.riverfronttimes.com/dailyrft/2014/02/high-tech_workshop_where_jack_dorsey_jim_mckelvey_built_square_eyeing_st_louis.php.

[50] GigaOm, "Square doubles in size in a year; now boasts 600 employees," October 7, 2013. http://gigaom.com/2013/10/07/square-doubles-in-size-in-a-year-now-boasting-600-employees/.

[51] Businessweek, "TechShop: Paradise for Tinkerers," May 23, 2012. http://www.businessweek.com/articles/2012-05-23/techshop-paradise-for-tinkerers#p1.

[52] http://www.ideaslaboratory.com/2014/02/06/welcome-to-the-era-of-the-hardware-startup/

[53] Strategy&, "America's Real Manufacturing Advantage," Spring 2014. http://www.strategy-business.com/media/file/00240_Americas_Real_Manufacturing_Advantage.pdf.

[54] Strategy&, "America's Real Manufacturing Advantage," Spring 2014. http://www.strategy-business.com/media/file/00240_Americas_Real_Manufacturing_Advantage.pdf.

[55] For an example of this, please see: http://www.dell.com/learn/us/en/555/videos~en/documents~kristen-billhardt-hpc-in-manufacturing.aspx

[56] Manufacturing Weekly, "The game-changing technology that's transforming manufacturing," January 31, 2014. http://www.manufacturingweekly.com/supercomputers/.

[57] HPC Wire. *Super Computers Boost Jet Engine Design.* http://www.hpcwire.com/2014/06/11/supercomputers-boost-jet-engine-design/

[58] Trop, Jaclyn. "Detroit, Embracing New Auto Technologies, Seeks App Builders." *The New York Times.* June 30, 2013.

[59] McKinsey Global Institute. *Disruptive Technologies: Advances that Will Transform Life, Business, and the Global Economy.* May 2013.

[60] Tassey, Gregory. *Rationales and mechanisms for revitalizing US Manufacturing R&D strategies.* NIST, 2010

[61] Congressional Research Service. *U.S. Manufacturing in International Perspective.* February 20, 2014.

[62] Bureau of Economic Analysis

[63] Bureau of Economic Analysis

[64] National Science Foundation, Science and Engineering Statistics

[65] Bureau of Economic Analysis

[66] U.S. Census, Business Dynamics Statistics.

[67] Bureau of Labor Statistics, Current Employment Statistics

[68] Interviews with Shapeways

[69] Interviews with Kickstarter

[70] Interviews with Quirky

[71] Office of Management and Budget, R&D Cross-Cut

[72] Helper, Susan and Kuan, Jenny. 2012. *Overcoming Collective Action Problems in the Automotive Supply Chain.* Connect Innovation Institute White Paper: Project on Production Innovation.

End